JUNIOR BIOS

W9-CIG-305

Jordan Fisher

BY NORA GARDINER

Enslow
PUBLISHING

Please visit our website, www.enslow.com. For a free color catalog of all our high-quality books, call toll free 1-800-398-2504 or fax 1-877-980-4454.

Library of Congress Cataloging-in-Publication Data

Names: Gardiner, Nora, author.
Title: Jordan Fisher / Nora Gardiner.
Description: New York : Enslow Publishing, [2022] | Series: Junior bios | Includes index.
Identifiers: LCCN 2020036877 (print) | LCCN 2020036878 (ebook) | ISBN 9781978525368 (library binding) | ISBN 9781978525344 (paperback) | ISBN 9781978525351 (set) | ISBN 9781978525375 (ebook)
Subjects: LCSH: Fisher, Jordan--Juvenile literature. | African American entertainers--Biography--Juvenile literature. | African American singers--Biography--Juvenile literature.
Classification: LCC PN2287.F497 G37 2022 (print) | LCC PN2287.F497 (ebook) | DDC 791.4502/8092 [B]--dc23
LC record available at https://lccn.loc.gov/2020036877
LC ebook record available at https://lccn.loc.gov/2020036878

First Edition

Published in 2022 by
Enslow Publishing
29 E. 21st Street
New York, NY 10010

Copyright © 2022 Enslow Publishing

Designer: Deanna Paternostro
Editor: Kate Mikoley

Photo credits: Cover, p. 1 (Jordan Fisher) VALERIE MACON/Contributor/AFP/Getty Images; cover, p. 1 (photo frame) Aleksandr Andrushkiv/Shutterstock.com; marble texture used throughout HardtIllustrations/Shutterstock.com; lined paper texture used throughout Mtsaride/Shutterstock.com; watercolor texture used throughout solarbird/Shutterstock.com; p. 5 Young Hollywood/Contributor/Getty Images Entertainment/Getty Images; p. 7 Jeffrey Mayer/Contributor/WireImage/Getty Images; p. 9 Rodrigo Vaz/Contributor/FilmMagic/Getty Images; pp. 10, 17 FOX/Contributor/FOX Image Collection/Getty Images; pp. 13, 19 Walter McBride/Contributor/Getty Images Entertainment/Getty Images; p. 15 David Livingston/Contributor/Getty Images Entertainment/Getty Images.

Printed in the United States of America

Some of the images in this book illustrate individuals who are models. The depictions do not imply actual situations or events.

CPSIA compliance information: Batch #CWENS22: For further information contact Enslow Publishing, New York, New York, at 1-800-398-2504.

Find us on

 Contents

Words in the glossary appear in **bold** type
the first time they are used in the text.

A Man of Many Talents

Jordan Fisher has a following in just about every corner of the entertainment world. He's been on TV, in movies, and on Broadway. He's put out albums and has an active Twitch channel.

Jordan was born April 24, 1994, in Birmingham, Alabama. He was raised by his grandparents, who officially **adopted** him in 2005. As a child, he played soccer and did gymnastics. He first joined the drama club in fifth grade because he had a crush on a girl!

JORDAN TOLD THE STORY OF HIS ADOPTION WHEN HE APPEARED ON *DANCING WITH THE STARS* IN 2017. HE CALLS HIS GRANDPARENTS "MOM" AND "DAD."

FACTS BEHIND THE FIGURE

Jordan has a younger brother and sister who were also adopted by their grandparents.

Just Starting Out

Soon, Jordan was taking classes and acting with the Red Mountain Theatre Company. He was in *Dreamgirls*, *A Christmas Carol*, and *The Music Man*, among many other shows. He made his first trip to Los Angeles, California, at age 13. He knew he wanted to make acting and performing his job!

Jordan got his first **professional** acting jobs in 2009. He appeared on the Nickelodeon show *iCarly* and a web series called *The Hustler*. Jordan moved to Los Angeles full time at age 17.

ICARLY WAS JUST THE START OF JORDAN'S APPEARANCES ON WELL-LOVED TV SHOWS.

Break-Out *Star*

Jordan's big break on TV came in 2012 with a **role** on *The Secret Life of the American Teenager*. He followed that up with *Teen Beach Movie*, a TV movie in which he played Seacat. Fans loved him!

FACTS BEHIND THE FIGURE

Jordan appeared in *Teen Beach 2* in 2015 and sang a song on the **soundtrack**. He sang on *Liv and Maddie* too!

cast of *Teen Beach Movie*

JORDAN PLAYS MANY INSTRUMENTS,
INCLUDING PIANO, GUITAR, AND EVEN HARMONICA!

But it was the Disney Channel show *Liv and Maddie* that made Jordan Fisher a star. He started playing Holden on the show in 2015. He also got a record deal with Hollywood Records that year and started working on an album.

JORDAN BOTH SANG AND PLAYED GUITAR IN *GREASE: LIVE!*

The year 2016 was the biggest yet in Jordan's **career**. He appeared in *Grease: Live!* as Doody. He sang "These Magic Changes," which many people thought was one of the best parts of the show.

Jordan also recorded a remix of the song "You're Welcome" for the soundtrack of the Disney movie *Moana*. Not only that, he recorded it with Lin-Manuel Miranda, a hero of his. Jordan put out other music too. His **EP**, *Jordan Fisher*, came out in August 2016.

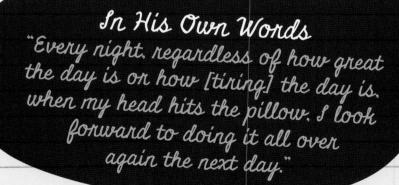

In His Own Words

"Every night, regardless of how great the day is or how [tiring] the day is, when my head hits the pillow, I look forward to doing it all over again the next day."

Broadway Debut

Grease: Live! opened the door to Broadway for Jordan. It was directed by Thomas Kail, who also directed the Broadway hit *Hamilton: An American Musical.* Kail asked Jordan to join the cast of *Hamilton!*

FACTS BEHIND THE FIGURE

Jordan got a tattoo of Founding Father Alexander Hamilton in honor of his time in *Hamilton.*

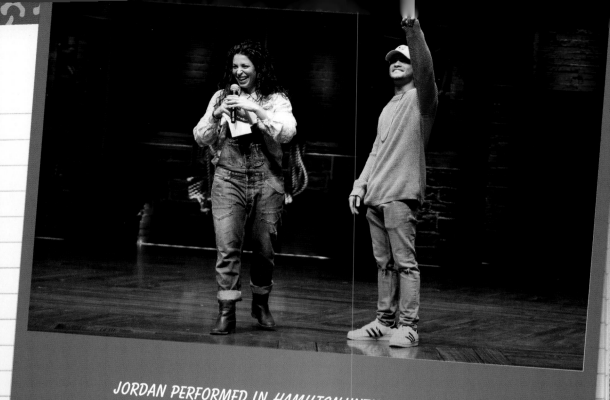

JORDAN PERFORMED IN HAMILTON UNTIL MARCH 5, 2017.

Jordan saw the show each night and **rehearsed** for hours a day for more than a month. Then, on November 22, 2016, Jordan made his Broadway **debut**! He took over the role of John Laurens/Philip Hamilton. Later, he said the first night in *Hamilton* was a "blur."

13

Dancing to the Top

Soon after Jordan left *Hamilton*, *Liv and Maddie* also finished airing. However, he found the perfect place to show off his many talents next: *Dancing with the Stars*!

His time on the show began in September 2017. Jordan and his partner, Lindsay Arnold, were favorites to win throughout the season. They earned perfect scores from judges and excited fans with their dances. One of the judges called Jordan "the most complete male **celebrity** ever on *Dancing with the Stars*." Jordan and Lindsay won!

JORDAN AND LINDSAY ALSO PERFORMED TOGETHER ON THE *DANCING WITH THE STARS* LIVE TOUR!

FACTS BEHIND THE FIGURE

Jordan became the youngest male winner of *Dancing with the Stars* when he and Lindsay Arnold won.

Jordan's win on *Dancing with the Stars* led him to host *Dancing with the Stars: Juniors* in 2018. That year, he also started voicing Sea Hawk and other characters on *She-Ra and the Princesses of Power*. He would go on to voice Finly on *Archibald's Next Big Thing* too.

Jordan took on another big challenge in 2019: the role of Mark Cohen in *Rent: Live*. He was the first Black actor to play the part in a major performance of the show!

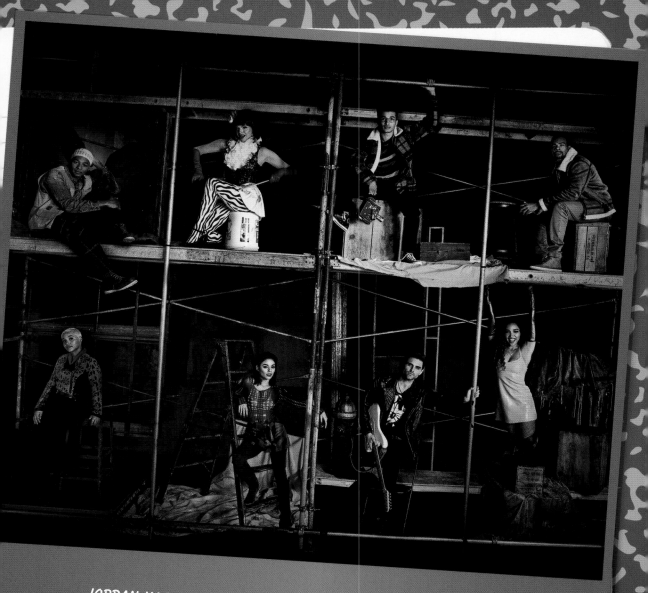

JORDAN HAS CALLED MARK COHEN IN *RENT* HIS "DREAM ROLE."

A Starring Role

In January 2020, Jordan returned to Broadway as the first Black Evan in *Dear Evan Hansen*. The part was hard to learn, and Jordan worked with a voice coach to sing it. He said he found the hard work to be the most **rewarding** of his career.

In His Own Words

"For any person of color to come into the theater and sit down and see somebody that they can **relate** to ... and then start to dig deep with this person and feel less alone ... feel like they belong. it's a very powerful thing."

JORDAN'S TIME IN *DEAR EVAN HANSEN* WAS CUT SHORT WHEN BROADWAY SHOWS WERE SHUT DOWN DURING THE COVID-19 **PANDEMIC.**

Jordan also starred in movies for Netflix. He earned new fans for playing John Ambrose in *To All the Boys: P.S. I Still Love You.* Then, he showed off his dance skills again in *Work It.*

Gamer Go-Getter

Jordan has become well known for other screen work too. He's a big gamer with an active Twitch channel. There, he streams games and talks to fans and fellow gamers. Jordan even cohosted the *Fortnite* World Cup in 2019.

Jordan is open to whatever the future holds for him: "I have crafted a world in the last 16 years of doing this where I've never really had to pick one thing over the other, and thankfully I love all of the things that I do."

FACTS BEHIND THE FIGURE

In May 2019, Jordan asked his girlfriend, Ellie Woods, to marry him. They got married in Disney World in November 2020!

Jordan's Timeline

1994: JORDAN IS BORN ON APRIL 24 IN BIRMINGHAM, ALABAMA.

2005: HE IS ADOPTED BY HIS GRANDPARENTS.

2009: JORDAN APPEARS ON *ICARLY*.

2012: HE BEGINS APPEARING ON *THE SECRET LIFE OF THE AMERICAN TEENAGER*.

2013: JORDAN IS IN *TEEN BEACH MOVIE*.

2015: HE STARTS WORKING ON *LIV AND MADDIE*. HE SIGNS A RECORD DEAL.

2016: JORDAN APPEARS IN *GREASE: LIVE!* HE MAKES HIS BROADWAY DEBUT IN *HAMILTON*.

2017: HE WINS *DANCING WITH THE STARS*.

2019: JORDAN PLAYS MARK COHEN IN *RENT: LIVE*. HE AND ELLIE GET ENGAGED.

2020: HE STARS IN *DEAR EVAN HANSEN* ON BROADWAY. HE APPEARS IN *TO ALL THE BOYS: P.S. I STILL LOVE YOU* AND *WORK IT*. JORDAN AND ELLIE GET MARRIED.

Glossary

adopt To make part of a family.

career The job someone chooses to do for a long time.

celebrity A person who is famous.

debut A first appearance.

EP A music recording that has more tracks than a single but not enough to be called an album. EP stands for extended play.

pandemic A time in which a disease spreads quickly to many places and affects many people in an area or throughout the world.

professional Earning money for an activity.

rehearse To prepare for a play or performance by practicing what will be performed.

relate To understand and like someone.

rewarding Giving a good feeling that one has done something important and of value.

role A part a person plays.

soundtrack The music used in a TV show or movie.

For More Information

Books

Pasek, Benj and Justin Paul. *You Will Be Found*. New York, NY: Little, Brown and Company, 2020.

Schwartz, Heather. *Lin-Manuel Miranda: Revolutionary Playwright, Composer, and Actor*. Minneapolis, MN: Lerner Publications, 2020.

Websites

Jordan Fisher
www.jordanfisherofficial.com/
Check out what's new with Jordan Fisher on his official website.

Jordan Fisher Twitch
www.twitch.tv/jordanfisher
Watch Jordan stream on Twitch here!

★ Index ★